FRUIT

HAMLYN

COOK'S NOTES

OVEN TEMPERATURES

°C	°F	GAS MARK	
70 C	150 F	Low	–
80 C	175 F	Low	–
90 C	190 F	Low	–
100 C	200 F	¼	–
110 C	225 F	¼	Very slow
130 C	250 F	½	Very slow
150 C	275 F	1	Slow
160 C	300 F	2	Moderately slow
170 C	325 F	3	Moderately slow
180 C	350 F	4	Moderate
190 C	375 F	5	Moderately hot
200 C	400 F	6	Hot
220 C	425 F	7	Hot
230 C	450 F	8	Very hot
240 C	475 F	9	Very hot

MICROWAVE POWER SETTINGS

Power Level	Percentage	Numerical Setting
HIGH	100%	9
MEDIUM HIGH	75%	7
MEDIUM	50%	5
DEFROST	30%	3
LOW	10%	1

SOLID WEIGHT CONVERSIONS

METRIC	IMPERIAL
15 g	½ oz
25 g	1 oz
50 g	2 oz
100 g	4 oz/¼ lb
175 g	6 oz
225 g	8 oz/½ lb
350 g	12 oz
450 g	1 lb
575 g	1¼ lb
700 g	1½ lb
800 g	1¾ lb
900 g	2 lb

MICROWAVE

Microwave tips have been tested using a 650 watt microwave oven. Add 15 seconds per minute for 600 watt ovens and reduce the timings by 5-10 seconds per minute for 700 watt ovens.

LIQUID VOLUME CONVERSIONS

METRIC	IMPERIAL
25 ml	1 fl oz
50 ml	2 fl oz
125 ml	4 fl oz
150 ml	5 fl oz/¼ pt
175 ml	6 fl oz
225 ml	8 fl oz
300 ml	10 fl oz/½ pt
450 ml	15 fl oz/¾ pt
600 ml	20 fl oz/1pt
900 ml	1½ pt
1.2 l	2 pt
1.7 l	3 pt

AUSTRALIAN CUP CONVERSIONS

	METRIC	IMP
1 cup flour	150 g	5 oz
1 cup sugar, granulated	225 g	8 oz
1 cup sugar, caster	225 g	8 oz
1 cup sugar, icing	175 g	6 oz
1 cup sugar, soft brown	175 g	6 oz
1 cup butter	225 g	8 oz
1 cup honey, treacle	350 g	12 oz
1 cup fresh breadcrumbs	50 g	2 oz
1 cup uncooked rice	200 g	7 oz
1 cup dried fruit	175 g	6 oz
1 cup chopped nuts	100 g	4 oz
1 cup desiccated coconut	75 g	3 oz
1 cup liquid	250 ml	9 fl oz

WEIGHTS AND MEASURES

Metric and Imperial weights and measures are given throughout. Don't switch from one to the other within a recipe as they are not interchangeable. 1 tsp is the equivalent of a 5 ml spoon and 1 tbls equals a 15 ml spoon.
All spoon measurements are level, all flour plain, all sugar granulated and all eggs medium unless otherwise stated.

SYMBOLS

 FREEZER TIP

 SERVING SUGGESTION

 MICRO-WAVE TIP

 WINE & DRINK NOTE

CONTENTS

First published in Great Britain 1993
by Hamlyn
an imprint of Reed Consumer Books Limited
Michelin House, 81 Fulham Road, London SW3 6RB
and Auckland, Melbourne, Singapore and Toronto

ISBN 0 600 57773 2

A CIP catalogue for this book is available at the British Library

Produced by Mandarin Offset
Printed and Bound in Singapore

EXOTIC FRUIT SALAD

Alan Newnham

Take advantage of the exotic fruit now widely available from major supermarkets and speciality shops. Don't hesitate to experiment and your dessert is bound to be a success.

PREPARATION TIME: 30 MINS +
CHILLING
COOKING TIME: 10 MINS
SERVES 8

INGREDIENTS

12 CHINESE GOOSEBERRIES

2 PASSION FRUIT

1 STAR FRUIT

1 BANANA, PEELED AND SLICED

6 STRAWBERRIES, HULLED AND HALVED

SMALL BUNCH OF SEEDLESS BLACK GRAPES

100 G/4 OZ RED CHERRIES

FOR THE SYRUP

3 CARDAMOM PODS

3 SPRIGS OF MINT

JUICE OF ½ A LEMON

1 CINNAMON STICK

¼ TSP CHINESE SPICES

75 G/3 OZ SUGAR

2 Peel back the outer casing from the Chinese gooseberries and place the fruit in a glass bowl. Halve the passion fruit and scoop out the pulp; add to the bowl. Slice the star fruit horizontally and add to the bowl. Stir in the banana, strawberries, grapes and cherries and strain over the cold syrup. Add the reserved mint sprigs to the bowl and chill the salad well before serving.

TIP

CHINESE SPICES IS ALSO KNOWN AS 5-SPICE POWDER AND IS MADE UP OF A COMBINATION OF INGREDIENTS: EQUAL PARTS OF GROUND ANISE, STAR ANISE, CINNAMON, CLOVES AND FENNEL SEEDS.

 SERVE THIS FRUIT SALAD JUST AS IT IS, CREAM WILL ONLY SERVE TO MASK THE FLAVOUR. IF WISHED, DESSERT BIS-CUITS LIKE *LANGUES-DU-CHAT* OR BOUDOIR CAN BE SERVED AS AN ACCOMPANIMENT TO THE FRUIT SALAD.

1 First make the syrup: lightly crush the cardamom pods with a knife so they split to release their flavour. Strip the leaves from the mint sprigs and reserve the best of them. Put the stalks, larger mint leaves, cardamom pods, lemon juice, cinnamon stick and Chinese spices with the sugar and 300 ml/½ pt water in a pan and bring very slowly to the boil. Leave the mixture until cold.

 PUT ALL THE SYRUP INGRE-DIENTS IN A MICROWAVE-PROOF BOWL. COVER AND COOK ON MEDIUM HIGH (75%) FOR 5 MINUTES OR UNTIL BOILING.

INDIVIDUAL SUMMER PUDDINGS

Paul Moon

The epitome of a summer dessert – fruity and refreshing. They look stunning but are made quite simply in teacups.

PREPARATION TIME: 30 MINS
+ CHILLING
COOKING TIME: 10 MINS
SERVES 6

I N G R E D I E N T S

1 LOAF SLICED WHITE BREAD,
CRUSTS REMOVED

900 G/2 LB MIXED SOFT FRUIT
(RASPBERRIES, REDCURRANTS,
PLUMS)

75 G/3 OZ CASTER SUGAR

FOR THE DECORATION

50 ML/2 FL OZ DOUBLE CREAM

6 SPRIGS OF REDCURRANTS

3 Lift the fruit out of the juice and sugar mixture and pack into the cups. Cut 6 circles from the reserved bread slices and use to cover the fruit. Sprinkle with half the fruit juice. Reserve the rest of the juice.

4 Cover filled cups with greaseproof paper. Stand on a tray and put a ramekin with a small weight inside, on top of each one. Chill in the fridge overnight.

5 Turn out the puddings onto 6 dessert plates and surround with a pool of the reserved juice. Pipe 2 rings of cream around each pudding and feather with a skewer.

1 Cut 6 circles of bread to line the base of each teacup. Cut strips for the sides, reserving 6 slices.

2 Halve and stone the fruit where necessary. Cook gently with the sugar until the juices flow.

HEAT FRUIT AND SUGAR ON HIGH (100%) FOR 7-8 MINUTES, STIRRING TWICE.

STRAWBERRY & VANILLA MOUSSE

Ian O'Leary

A marbled mousse of strawberries and cream set in a pool of strawberry purée feathered with double cream. If strawberries are not available, use raspberries, adding a little icing sugar to the purée if necessary.

PREPARATION TIME: 30 MINS
+ CHILLING
COOKING TIME: 2 MINS
SERVES 6

I N G R E D I E N T S

175 G/6 OZ STRAWBERRIES

4 EGGS, SEPARATED

100 G/4 OZ CASTER SUGAR

250 ML/9 FL OZ DOUBLE CREAM

FEW DROPS OF VANILLA ESSENCE

6 TSP (1 ½ SACHETS) POWDERED
GELATINE

2-3 SLICED STRAWBERRIES, TO
DECORATE

MINT LEAVES, TO DECORATE

FOR THE SAUCE

100 G/4 OZ STRAWBERRIES

1 TSP ARROWROOT

25 G/1 OZ ICING SUGAR

1 Purée the strawberries in a food processor. Transfer to a bowl and set aside. Whisk the egg yolks and caster sugar until pale and thick enough to leave a trail when the whisk is lifted.

2 In separate bowls, whip the cream to soft peaks and whisk the egg whites until stiff. Fold the cream and then the egg whites into the egg yolk mixture. Fold 5 tbls of the egg mixture into the strawberry purée. Stir vanilla essence into the remaining egg mixture.

3 Sprinkle the gelatine over 6 tbls of warm water in a bowl and set aside to soften for a few minutes. Then stir and place over a pan of warm water to dissolve.

4 Fold 4 tbls of the gelatine mixture into the vanilla egg mixture and stir the remainder into the strawberry purée mixture.

5 Pour half of the vanilla mousse mixture into a 1.2 L/2 pt ring mould and swirl in half the strawberry mixture. Add the remaining vanilla and strawberry mixture and swirl again. Chill for 1½-2 hours.

6 Make the sauce: purée the strawberries, shake the arrowroot into 1 tbls water and stir into the purée. Add the icing sugar and stir over a gentle heat until glossy and slightly thickened. Allow to cool. Unmould the mousse, slice and put on serving plates. Surround with sauce. Feather in the cream using a cocktail stick. Decorate with strawberries and mint leaves.

APRICOT MERINGUE JELLY

Alan Newnham

This dish has an unusual but quite delicious
centre of jelly made from a purée of apricots.
Tiny meringues make a decorative finish.

PREPARATION TIME: 45 MINS
+ SOAKING
COOKING TIME: 1 HOUR 5 MINS-
1 HOUR 35 MINS
SERVES 4

I N G R E D I E N T S

1 EGG WHITE

50 G/2 OZ CASTER SUGAR

1 DROP OF VANILLA ESSENCE

FOR THE JELLY

225 G/8 OZ DRIED APRICOTS

JUICE OF ½ A LEMON

135 G/4¾ OZ ORANGE JELLY

150 ML/¼ PT DOUBLE CREAM,
WHIPPED

FRESH OR TINNED APRICOTS, TO
DECORATE

1 To make the meringues, preheat the oven to 100 C/200 F/Gas ¼. Whisk the egg white until stiff and shiny then fold in sugar and vanilla essence. If using a hand whisk, add 1 tsp of sugar and the vanilla essence, before folding in remaining sugar. Line a baking tray with baking parchment.

2 Spoon the mixture into a plain-nozzled piping bag and pipe small meringues onto the parchment making sure the meringues are kept far apart from each other. Bake for ¾-1¼ hours or until the meringues are dry. Lift off the parchment and cool on a wire rack. Store until needed.

3 To make the jelly: put the apricots and 300 ml/½ pt water into a saucepan and bring to the boil. Remove and leave the apricots to soak for 1 hour. Return to the heat, cover and cook slowly for 20 minutes or until the apricots are soft. Remove the apricots with a slotted spoon and reserve liquid. Purée the apricots together with the lemon juice and add water to make up purée to 300 ml/½ pt. Pour the apricot liquid into a measuring jug and make up to 300 ml/½ pt by adding boiling water to the jug.

4 Break the orange jelly into pieces and stir into the liquid. Once dissolved, mix thoroughly with the apricot purée and pour into a shallow round dish or cake tin and leave to set in the fridge.

5 Once the jelly has set turn out onto a plate and spread with whipped cream over the jelly. Decorate with the meringues and slices of apricots.

PEACH MELBA

Clint Brown

Melba sauce was created by the chef,
Escoffier, at the end of the last century for the
Australian opera singer, Dame Nellie Melba.
Here is an elegant version of a classic recipe.

PREPARATION TIME: 15 MINS +
CHILLING
SERVES 4

I N G R E D I E N T S

450 G/1 LB FRESH OR THAWED
FROZEN RASPBERRIES

100 G/4 OZ ICING SUGAR

4 PEACHES

4 SCOOPS OF VANILLA ICE CREAM, TO
SERVE

10-20 seconds to loosen the skins, then remove the peaches with a slotted spoon. Use a small, sharp knife to help remove the peach skins.

1 Place the raspberries in a fine nylon sieve set over a large bowl. Push the fruit through the sieve with a spatula and discard any pips that are left in the sieve.

2 Beat the icing sugar into the raspberry purée. Taste and add more sugar if necessary. Chill in the fridge until required.

4 Cut the peaches into quarters and remove the stones. Make 2 V-shaped cuts, one smaller than the other, without cutting right through the peach, to make 3 small wedges. Push the wedges half out. Pour the melba sauce onto 4 dessert plates and arrange 4 peach segments on each. Place a scoop of ice cream in the centre to serve.

TIP

FOR A SPECIAL OCCASION ADD 2 TBLS OF KIRSCH OR FRAMBOISE TO THE MELBA SAUCE AND, IF WISHED, DECORATE WITH TOASTED ALMONDS OR MINT.

3 Place the peaches in a large, heatproof bowl and pour over boiling water to cover. Leave for

BLACKCURRANT SHORTCAKE

Paul Moon

A variation on the classic strawberry shortcake – this one is filled with a creamy blackcurrant mousse and topped with wedges of shortcake.

PREPARATION TIME: 30 MINS +
CHILLING
COOKING TIME: 25 MINS
SERVES 8

INGREDIENTS

150 G/5 OZ FLOUR
150 G/5 OZ GROUND ALMONDS
175 G/6 OZ BUTTER
50 G/2 OZ CASTER SUGAR
25 G/1 OZ CHOPPED NUTS
1 TBLS ICING SUGAR
FOR THE MOUSSE
450 G/1 LB BLACKCURRANTS
4 TSP (1 SACHET) GELATINE
2 EGGS, SEPARATED
50 G/2 OZ CASTER SUGAR
300 ML/½ PT DOUBLE CREAM, LIGHTLY WHIPPED

1 Preheat the oven to 180 C/350 F/ Gas 4. Sift the flour into a bowl and stir in the ground almonds. Rub in the butter, stir in the sugar and bring the mixture together to make a firm dough. Halve the dough and press one half onto a baking tray. Cut out a circle using a 20 cm/8 in spring-form tin. Sprinkle over the chopped nuts.

2 Press the remaining dough into the bottom of a 20 cm/8 in spring-form tin. Bake both rounds for 25 minutes until golden. Cool slightly then cut the round on the baking tray into 8 equal, triangular wedges.

3 Pick over the blackcurrants and reserve 9 good ones for decoration. Strig the remaining blackcurrants (remove from stalks) and place the berries in a pan with 4 tbls water. Bring to the boil, cover and simmer for 5 minutes until softened. Rub the fruit through a sieve. Sprinkle the gelatine over 4 tbls water in a small pan, stir and leave until spongy – about 5 minutes. Stir over low heat until dissolved. Whisk the egg yolks and sugar together until pale and creamy. Stir the purée into the yolks with the dissolved gelatine.

4 Whisk the egg whites to form soft peaks and fold into the mixture with three-quarters of the cream.

5 Line the sides of the tin with baking parchment, pour in the mousse over the shortcake and chill for 2-3 hours until set. Remove the mousse from the tin and put on a serving plate. Use the remaining cream to pipe 8 rosettes evenly around the top. Arrange the wedges at an angle on the cream. Pipe more cream rosettes on the shortcake and decorate with the blackcurrants. Sift the icing sugar over the top if wished.

BLUEBERRY CHEESECAKE

Clint Brown

The tangy taste of blueberries combines with the rich flavour of cream to make this cheesecake irresistible. Serve it to impress.

PREPARATION TIME: 20 MINS
+ CHILLING
COOKING TIME: 2 MINS
SERVES 6-8

INGREDIENTS

FOR THE BASE

175 G/6 OZ SHORTBREAD BISCUITS, CRUSHED

50 G/2 OZ GROUND ALMONDS

75 G/3 OZ MELTED BUTTER, PLUS EXTRA FOR GREASING

FOR THE FILLING

225 G/8 OZ CREAM CHEESE

50 G/2 OZ CASTER SUGAR

1 EGG, SEPARATED

150 ML/¼ PT DOUBLE CREAM

275 G/10 OZ BOTTLED BLUEBERRIES, DRAINED

2 TSP GELATINE

FOR THE DECORATION

150 ML/¼ PT DOUBLE CREAM

24 FRESH BLUEBERRIES

FRESH MINT LEAVES

fold in. Purée the blueberries and stir into the cream cheese mixture until it is well combined.

2 Sprinkle the gelatine over 4 tbls water. Leave to soak for 5 minutes, then dissolve over a pan of simmering water until completely clear. Allow to cool then stir into the blueberry and cheese mixture.

3 Whisk the egg white until it forms soft peaks then gently fold into the blueberry mixture.

4 Pour the cheesecake mixture into the prepared tin and place in the fridge for 2½-3 hours or until sèt. Before serving, whip the double cream until thick. Remove the cheesecake from the tin and decorate with cream rosettes, blueberries and mint leaves.

TIP

USE A PIPING BAG AND STAR-SHAPED NOZZLE TO APPLY THE WHIPPED CREAM DECORATION. THE PRETTY EFFECT IS WELL WORTH THE EXTRA EFFORT.

1 Mix the crushed biscuits and ground almonds together with the melted butter. Lightly grease and line the base of a 23 cm/9 in spring-form tin. Press the biscuit mixture into the tin. Chill in the fridge for 30 minutes. Beat the cream cheese, sugar and egg yolk together until smooth. Lightly whip the cream and

BLUEBERRY CHARLOTTE

Peter Smith

Here's a dish made using only five ingredients.
The finished dessert is often tied with a satin
ribbon round its middle.

PREPARATION TIME: 15 MINS
+ CHILLING
COOKING TIME: 2 MINS
SERVES 6

I N G R E D I E N T S

400 G/14 OZ TINNED BLUEBERRIES
IN SYRUP

ABOUT 25 G/1 OZ (¼ PACKET)
BLACKCURRANT JELLY

21 SPONGE FINGER BISCUITS

900 G/2 LB QUARK

4 TSP (1 SACHET) POWDERED
GELATINE

1 Drain the blueberries, reserving the syrup. Spoon 3 tbls of the syrup into a bowl and set aside. Pour the rest into a jug, add the jelly and enough water to make up to 150 ml/¼ pt. Heat in a pan until dissolved.

2 Pour the jelly into a charlotte mould. Carefully stir in 2 tbls blueberries and chill in the fridge until set.

4 Process the remaining fruit in a food processor with a little of the quark, then rub through a sieve. Return to the washed food processor, add the remaining quark and process the mixture until smooth.

5 Sprinkle the gelatine over the reserved syrup and leave until spongy. Set the bowl over simmering water and stir until dissolved. Cool then add to the cheese and fruit mixture. Process again.

3 Carefully trim the sides of the finger biscuits and use them to line the slightly sloping sides of the charlotte mould, sugared side outwards. Chill for 30 minutes.

6 Spoon into the mould and chill for 30 minutes. Trim the tops of the sponge fingers if necessary so they are level with the filling. Dip base of mould in hot water, place a plate over the top and invert, giving it a sharp shake.

 SERVE WITH LIGHTLY-WHIPPED CREAM OR A SCOOP OF VANILLA ICE CREAM.

MINTED APPLES & PEARS

Ian O'Leary

A sumptuous fresh fruit dessert to end
a dinner party – apples and pears on a filo
pastry base topped with a mint and lemon-
flavoured syrup.

PREPARATION TIME: 20 MINS
COOKING TIME: 30 MINS
SERVES 4

I N G R E D I E N T S

2 SHEETS OF FILO PASTRY

50 G/2 OZ BUTTER, MELTED

2 PEARS

2 DESSERT APPLES

PARED RIND AND JUICE OF 1 LEMON

75 G/3 OZ SUGAR

1 BLADE OF MACE

2 MINT SPRIGS

6 CRACKED CARDAMOM PODS

4 MINT SPRIGS, TO GARNISH

FOR THE CARAMEL SYRUP

175 G/6 OZ CASTER SUGAR

3 Place the pears and apples in another pan and strain the syrup over. Reserve the lemon rind. Cover and simmer for 8-10 minutes or until all the fruit is tender. Drain. Cut the lemon rind into fine needle shreds.

1 Preheat the oven to 200 C/400 F/ Gas 6. Lay filo pastry out on a work surface. Brush one sheet with melted butter and top with the other. Brush with the remaining butter. Cut 4 circles or shapes to fit the bottoms of your serving plates. Place on a baking tray and bake for 10 minutes until golden brown. Allow the filo shapes to cool.

4 Bring 75 ml/3 fl oz water and the caster sugar to the boil in a pan, stirring until the sugar dissolves. Continue boiling for a further 3 minutes. Add the needle shreds and boil until the syrup is a light golden colour.

5 Arrange the filo on serving plates, top with 2 quarters of pears and 2 of apple, and spoon the caramel syrup over. Decorate with sprigs of mint.

2 Peel, quarter and core the pears and apples. Sprinkle with lemon juice. Boil 300 ml/½ pt water and the sugar, lemon rind, mace, mint and cardamom, stirring until the sugar dissolves. Simmer for 10 minutes.

TIP

PARE WIDE STRIPS OF RIND FROM THE LEMON USING A VEGETABLE PEELER. THIS WILL MAKE THE RIND EASIER TO RECOVER AND USE AGAIN AFTER COOKING WITH THE APPLES AND PEARS.

PLUM MOUSSE

Alan Newnham

Serve this light, subtle-flavoured mousse with
puréed plum sauce and crisp brandysnaps
curled into cylinders.

PREPARATION TIME: 10 MINS
+ CHILLING
SERVES 6

INGREDIENTS

900 G/2 LB PLUMS, STONED

3 TBLS ICING SUGAR, SIFTED

1 KG/2 LB 4 OZ FROMAGE FRAIS

3 TBLS PLUM JAM, SIEVED

8 TSP (2 SACHETS) POWDERED
GELATINE

ROSE-SCENTED GERANIUM LEAF,
TO DECORATE

3 To unmould: dip the base of the mould in hot water, hold a plate over the top and invert. Garnish with the reserved plum slices and rose-scented geranium leaf and serve with the remaining plum purée.

 TRY MAKING INDIVIDUAL MOUSSES BY DIVIDING THE PLUM MIXTURE BETWEEN 4 SMALL MOULDS. WHEN SET, PIPE ROSETTES OF WHIPPED CREAM ON TOP.

1 Blend the plums (reserving 3 slices for decoration). Sieve. Stir in the icing sugar.

2 Tip the fromage frais into a bowl and add the jam. Dissolve the gelatine in 2 tbls water over a gentle heat. Stir into the fromage frais. Add two-thirds of the purée. Pour into a 1.2 L/2 pt metal mould. Chill.

MANGO FOOL

Chris King

Add a Caribbean touch to your meal by serving
Mango Fool as a dessert. This colourful, tangy
dish exudes the spicy aroma of cloves.

PREPARATION TIME: 20 MINS +
CHILLING
SERVES 6-8

I N G R E D I E N T S

2 MANGOES

4 TBLS SWEET WHITE WINE

¼ TSP GROUND CLOVES

450 ML/¾ PT DOUBLE CREAM

PARED ORANGE ZEST, TO DECORATE

3 Spoon the mango mixture into a large serving bowl or 6-8 individual dishes. Pipe the reserved cream in rosettes over the top of the fool. Chill for 30 minutes, then decorate with the orange zest and serve.

TIP

IF YOU DON'T WANT TO OPEN A BOTTLE OF WINE FOR THIS DISH, USE 4 TBLS ORANGE JUICE INSTEAD. YOU CAN ALSO TRY MAKING THIS FOOL WITH SEVERAL DIFFERENT PURÉES AT ONCE, LAYERED ON TOP OF EACH OTHER, SUCH AS APRICOT, PEACH AND PASSION FRUIT.

 SERVE MANGO FOOL WITH SMALL PLAIN OR ALMOND-FLAVOURED BISCUITS.

1 Stand the mangoes on one end and cut the flesh off from around the stone. Cut through the flesh to the skin on the outer pieces and make squares. Turn the skin up to separate the flesh, then remove the flesh from the skin using a metal spoon. Alternatively, cut the mangoes into slices, remove the peel and roughly chop the flesh.

2 Purée the flesh with the sweet white wine and ground cloves. Whip the cream until thick. Reserve 4 tbls for the decoration and fold the rest into the purée mixture.

LEMON GERANIUM SYLLABUB

Infusing wine with lemon geranium leaves
gives this foamy syllabub a subtle flavour.
Serve with homemade dessert biscuits.

PREPARATION TIME: 25 MINS +
CHILLING
COOKING TIME: 5 MINS
SERVES 4

I N G R E D I E N T S

JUICE OF 1 LEMON

6 TBLS WHITE WINE

8 LEMON GERANIUM LEAVES

3 TBLS CASTER SUGAR

300 ML/½ PT DOUBLE CREAM

FOR THE BISCUITS

2 EGG WHITES

100 G/4 OZ CASTER SUGAR

100 G/4 OZ FLOUR

ZEST OF 1 ORANGE

FOR THE DECORATION

4 LEMON GERANIUM LEAVES

PARED LEMON RIND

2 Stir in the cream and whisk the mixture until it forms soft peaks. Spoon the mixture into 4 glasses and chill for 30 minutes. Decorate the syllabub with geranium leaves and pared lemon zest.

1 Place the lemon juice, white wine, geranium leaves and caster sugar in a bowl. Leave to infuse for 15 minutes then remove the leaves and discard them.

3 While the syllabub is chilling make the biscuits. Preheat the oven to 200 C/400 F/Gas 6. Whisk the egg whites and sugar together in a bowl until thick. Fold in the flour and orange zest. Pipe into small flower shapes onto baking parchment on a bàking tray. Bake for 4-5 minutes and leave to cool on a wire rack. Serve with the syllabub.

WATCHPOINT

SCENTED GERANIUM LEAVES (ROSE AND LEMON) ARE THE ONLY ONES RECOM-MENDED BY HERBALISTS FOR INFUSION IN COOKERY.

TIP

LEMON GERANIUM LEAVES ARE AVAIL-ABLE FROM HERBALISTS — SUPERMAR-KETS AND HEALTH FOOD SHOPS RARELY STOCK THEM.

MIXED COMPOTE

Light and deliciously refreshing, fruit compotes make the perfect finale to a meal. This version uses a mixture of dried and fresh autumn fruits.

Clive Streeter

PREPARATION TIME: 15 MINS
+ SOAKING
COOKING TIME: 15 MINS
SERVES 4

I N G R E D I E N T S

100 G/4 OZ DRIED APRICOTS
100 G/4 OZ DRIED PEACHES
½ SMALL PINEAPPLE
2 APPLES
1 LARGE NECTARINE
600 ML/1 PT APPLE JUICE
40 G/1 ½ OZ DEMERARA SUGAR
1 CINNAMON STICK
2 WHOLE CLOVES
STRAINED GREEK YOGHURT, TO SERVE

2 Peel the pineapple, slice into rings, remove and discard core. Cut into pieces. Peel, core and chop the apples and stone and chop the nectarine. Place in the pan.

Peter Reilly

3 Add the apple juice, sugar, cinnamon stick and cloves. Bring to the boil, stirring occasionally, then cover and simmer for 10 minutes or until the fruit is tender.

1 Place the apricots and peaches in a bowl, cover with water and soak overnight. Drain and cut apricots into halves and peaches into quarters. Place in a large saucepan.

4 Remove from heat and leave to cool. Turn into a serving dish and chill in the fridge for 1-2 hours. Serve with the strained Greek yoghurt.

m MICROWAVING IS VERY CONVENIENT AS THE COMPOTE CAN BE COOKED AND CHILLED IN THE SAME CONTAINER. PLACE FRUIT IN A NON-METALLIC BOWL, COVER WITH CLING FILM AND MICROWAVE ON HIGH (100%) FOR 10 MINUTES. STIR HALFWAY THROUGH COOKING TIME.

CARIBBEAN BANANAS

Bring some sunshine into your home by making this delicious tropical dessert. The special combination of juices, sugar, spices and rum is irresistible.

PREPARATION TIME: 5 MINS
COOKING TIME: 10 MINS
SERVES 4

INGREDIENTS

4 LARGE BANANAS

GRATED ZEST AND JUICE OF 1 ORANGE

PINCH OF GRATED NUTMEG

¼ TSP GROUND CINNAMON

3 TBLS SOFT BROWN SUGAR

75 ML/3 FL OZ DARK RUM

15 G/½ OZ BUTTER, MELTED

4 TBLS STRAINED GREEK YOGHURT OR WHIPPED CREAM, TO SERVE

TIP

FOR A CHANGE, ADD 4 HALVED SLICES OF FRESH PINEAPPLE, AND 75 ML/3 FL OZ MALIBU INSTEAD OF THE DARK RUM. SPRINKLE 3 TBLS DESICCATED COCONUT OVER THE TOP AND COOK ACCORDING TO THE RECIPE.

WATCHPOINT

DON'T CUT UP THE BANANAS AND LEAVE THEM FOR ANY LENGTH OF TIME AS THEY QUICKLY GO BROWN.

 TO COOK THIS DISH IN THE MICROWAVE, USE THE JUICE FROM 2 ORANGES, OMIT THE RUM, BLEND THE REST OF THE INGREDIENTS TOGETHER IN A MICROWAVE-PROOF DISH. COVER AND COOK ON HIGH (100%) FOR 2 MINUTES. POUR 1 TBLS RUM OVER THE BANANAS BEFORE SERVING WITH THE YOGHURT OR WHIPPED CREAM.

1 Preheat the oven to 190 C/375 F/ Gas 5. Peel the bananas, slice thickly on the diagonal and lay them in a shallow ovenproof dish.

2 Mix the remaining ingredients together and pour over the bananas. Bake for 10 minutes until golden and bubbling. Serve while still hot, topped with the yoghurt or cream.

UPSIDE-DOWN PEAR PUDDING

Clint Brown

They'll love you forever for this one! Topped with pears, this rich baked pudding is a heavenly combination of light lemony sponge and rich caramel topping.

PREPARATION TIME: 30 MINS

COOKING TIME: 55 MINS-1 HOUR
5 MINS

SERVES 6

INGREDIENTS

2 MEDIUM PEARS
200 G/7 OZ BUTTER
75 G/3 OZ DEMERARA SUGAR
2 TBLS GOLDEN SYRUP
175 G/6 OZ CASTER SUGAR
3 EGGS, SEPARATED
GRATED ZEST AND JUICE OF 1 LEMON
150 G/5 OZ SELF-RAISING FLOUR
CUSTARD OR FRESH CREAM, TO SERVE

gentle heat until the sugar has almost dissolved. Pour over the bottom and sides of a 1.4 L/2½ pt pudding basin.

3 When the caramel begins to set, arrange the pear slices around the sides of the pudding basin, sticking them to the sides with the caramel sauce. Place a round slice of pear in the middle, pushing down through the caramel with a wooden spoon.

4 Beat the remaining butter with the caster sugar until light and fluffy. Beat in the egg yolks and lemon zest and then gently stir in the flour and lemon juice. Whisk the egg whites until stiff but not dry and fold thoroughly into the mixture.

1 Preheat the oven to 170 C/325 F/ Gas 3. Peel the pears, cut in half and carefully scoop out the core. Cut lengthways into 1 cm/⅓ in slices and poach gently in boiling water for 3 minutes or until just tender. Drain.

5 Pour into the basin and smooth the top with a knife. Bake in the oven for 45-55 minutes. To test if the pudding is cooked, insert a thin metal skewer into the centre of the pudding – it should come out clean. Turn out onto a serving plate and serve hot with custard or fresh cream.

2 Melt 25 g/1 oz of the butter in a pan with the demerara sugar and golden syrup and cook over a

SWEET CHERRY PIE

Clint Brown

This mouth-watering pie, bursting with plump sweet cherries, is best served piping hot with cream or custard.

PREPARATION TIME: 20 MINS
+ RESTING
COOKING TIME: 30-35 MINS
SERVES 4-6

INGREDIENTS

225 G/8 OZ FLOUR
PLUS EXTRA FOR DUSTING

100 G/4 OZ BUTTER

GRATED ZEST OF 1 ORANGE

50 G/2 OZ CASTER SUGAR

1 EGG YOLK

450 G/1 LB STONED CHERRIES,
THAWED IF FROZEN

2 TBLS CORNFLOUR

50 G/2 OZ ICING SUGAR

1 EGG, BEATEN

1 Preheat the oven to 200 C/400 F/ Gas 6. Sift the flour in a mixing bowl and rub in the butter, until the mixture resembles fine breadcrumbs. Stir in the orange zest, sugar, egg yolk and 2 tbls water to form a soft dough.

2 Knead gently on a floured work surface. Cover the pastry with cling film and chill in the fridge.

4 Roll out the other half of the pastry. Brush the edges of pastry base with water and cover with the rolled out pastry. Seal and flute the edges. Brush the pastry with the beaten egg. Re-roll the trimmings and using a knife, cut out cherry shapes to decorate the lid of the pie. Brush again with beaten egg. Bake for 30-35 minutes, until golden.

TIP

FOR A CRUNCHY TOPPING, BRUSH THE TOP OF THE PIE WITH COLD WATER AND SPRINKLE WITH SUGAR 5 MINUTES BEFORE THE END OF COOKING TIME.

3 On a floured work surface roll out half the pastry to 6 mm/¼ in thick. Use to line a 20 cm/8 in pie dish. Pile up the cherries in the centre. Blend together the cornflour and sugar in a bowl, and sieve over the cherries.

SPICY CHERRY CLAFOUTIS

Clint Brown

This is a wonderful classic French pudding traditionally made from rich, plump cherries cooked in a light fluffy batter.

PREPARATION TIME: 15 MINS
COOKING TIME: 40-50 MINS
SERVES 6-8

I N G R E D I E N T S

BUTTER, FOR GREASING

3 LARGE EGGS

75 G/3 OZ CASTER SUGAR

½ TSP VANILLA ESSENCE

2 TBLS BRANDY

75 G/3 OZ FLOUR

300 ML/½ PT MILK

450 G/1 LB FRESH OR TINNED
CHERRIES, STONED

½ TSP GROUND CINNAMON

2 TBLS ICING SUGAR,
FOR DREDGING

3 Sift the flour and fold into the egg mixture with a metal spoon until evenly mixed. Then gradually stir in the milk.

1 Preheat the oven to 190 C/375 F/ Gas 5. Lightly grease a shallow ovenproof 1.2 L/2 pt dish.

4 Arrange the cherries in the prepared dish and sprinkle with cinnamon. Pour the batter over the cherries and bake for about 40-50 minutes or until golden brown and spongy to the touch.

5 Sift the icing sugar over the pudding and then serve it immediately while it's hot.

2 Whisk the eggs and sugar together until pale in colour, frothy in texture and trebled in volume. Add the vanilla essence and brandy to the egg mixture.

TIP

FOR A CHANGE, REPLACE THE CHERRIES
WITH OTHER SEASONAL FRUIT SUCH AS
STONED PLUMS OR APRICOTS, AND IN-
STEAD OF THE BRANDY ADD KIRSCH TO
THE BATTER.

APPLE CHARLOTTES

Simon Wheeler

Serve these portion-sized baked apple and breadcrumb towers with a dollop of smooth, cool yoghurt.

PREPARATION TIME: 20 MINS
COOKING TIME: 30 MINS
SERVES 4

I N G R E D I E N T S

25 G/1 OZ BUTTER

2 COOKING APPLES, PEELED, CORED
AND CHOPPED

¾ TSP GROUND CINNAMON

50 G/2 OZ DEMERARA SUGAR

100 G/4 OZ FRESH BREADCRUMBS

50 G/2 OZ CASTER SUGAR

OIL, FOR GREASING

150 ML/¼ PT NATURAL YOGHURT

thirds of the mixture into the bases and
press onto sides and bases to line.

3 Fill with apple mixture and then
sprinkle over the remaining
breadcrumb mixture and press
down firmly. Bake in the oven for 15-20
minutes or until golden brown on top.

4 Carefully turn out onto warmed
serving plates and serve with
yoghurt sprinkled with the
remaining cinnamon.

1 Preheat the oven to 190 C/375 F/
Gas 5. Melt the butter and add
apples, ½ tsp cinnamon and
demerara sugar. Cook over a gentle heat
for 10 minutes. Remove from heat.

 SAUTE APPLE SLICES IN BUT-
TER AND BROWN SUGAR UNTIL
GOLDEN. SERVE WITH THE
CHARLOTTES.

 PLACE BUTTER, APPLE, CIN-
NAMON AND SUGAR IN A
BOWL. COOK ON HIGH
(100%) FOR 2 MINUTES.
STIR AND COOK FOR A FUR-
THER 6 MINUTES. REMOVE
FROM THE OVEN. FILL LINED
RAMEKINS WITH THE APPLE
MIXTURE AND THEN SPRINKLE
OVER THE REMAINING BREAD-
CRUMB MIXTURE. COOK THE
CHARLOTTES ON HIGH
(100%) FOR 10 MINUTES.

 THESE CAN BE MADE IN AD-
VANCE AND FROZEN — EITHER
BEFORE OR AFTER COOKING —
FOR 6 MONTHS. DEFROST
BEFORE COOKING.

2 Mix the breadcrumbs and caster
sugar together. Lightly oil 4
dariole moulds. Sprinkle two-

SPICED PEACH PUDDING

JJ Crofton

This moist, spiced sponge filled with fresh peach halves, can be made in next to no time. It has a crunchy demerara topping that's great served with a blob of cream.

PREPARATION TIME: 15 MINS
COOKING TIME: 30 MINS
SERVES 4

INGREDIENTS

OIL, FOR GREASING

75 G/3 OZ BUTTER, SOFTENED

75 G/3 OZ CASTER SUGAR

2 SMALL EGGS

50 G/2 OZ SELF-RAISING FLOUR

25 G/1 OZ GROUND ALMONDS

1 ½ TSP GROUND CINNAMON

4 FRESH PEACHES, PEELED, STONED
AND HALVED

1 TBLS DEMERARA SUGAR

WHIPPED DOUBLE CREAM, TO SERVE

3 Spoon the mixture into the prepared dish and spread out. Arrange the peach halves over the top, curved side up, and push them into the pudding mixture.

1 Preheat the oven to 190 C/375 F/ Gas 5. Lightly oil a 23 cm/9 in round, shallow ovenproof dish.

2 Beat the butter and sugar together in a large mixing bowl until pale. Beat in the eggs, one at a time, until light and fluffy. Fold in the flour, ground almonds and 1 tsp cinnamon.

4 Mix the demerara sugar and the remaining cinnamon together in a bowl and sprinkle evenly over the pudding. Bake for 30 minutes until well risen and golden. Serve either hot or warm with the whipped cream.

THIS PUDDING CAN BE MADE
IN ADVANCE AND FROZEN FOR
UP TO 6 MONTHS.

TIP

THE PUDDING MAY BE COOKED IN A
ROUND CAKE TIN THE SAME SIZE AS THE
DISH. LINE THE BASE OF THE TIN WITH
GREASEPROOF PAPER.

CHOCOLATE & PEAR CRUMBLE

Clint Brown

This not-so-humble crumble has little chunks of milk chocolate hidden in the topping. Pears and plums cooked in cider give the filling added punch. Serve with lashings of cream.

PREPARATION TIME: 10 MINS

COOKING TIME: 25 MINS

SERVES 4-6

I N G R E D I E N T S

4 PEARS

4 PLUMS

50 ML/2 FL OZ DRY CIDER

FOR THE CRUMBLE

50 G/2 OZ BUTTER

100 G/4 OZ FLOUR

25 G/1 OZ CASTER SUGAR

50 G/2 OZ MILK CHOCOLATE BUTTONS

1 Preheat the oven to 200 C/400 F/ Gas 6. Peel, core and chop the pears into rough chunks. Peel, quarter and remove the stones from the plums. Put all the fruit into a large saucepan with the dry cider. Bring the fruit and liquid to the boil and poach over a gentle heat for 5 minutes to slightly soften the fruit.

3 Tip the fruit into a 1.2 L/2 pt ovenproof dish and cover with the crumble. Bake in the oven for 20 minutes, or until golden brown.

WATCHPOINT

DO NOT USE FRUIT WHICH IS TOO RIPE BECAUSE IT WILL BREAK DOWN TOO MUCH ON COOKING. IT IS BEST TO USE FRUIT WHICH IS SLIGHTLY UNDERRIPE AND FIRM IN THIS RECIPE.

TO FREEZE: WRAP THE DISH, UNBAKED, IN FOIL. IT WILL KEEP IN THE FREEZER FOR UP TO 3 MONTHS. COOK THE CRUMBLE STRAIGHT FROM THE FREEZER IN AN OVEN SET AT 200 C/400 F/GAS 6 FOR 40 MINUTES.

2 Meanwhile make the crumble, rub the butter into the flour and sugar until the mixture resembles breadcrumbs. Roughly chop the buttons and stir into the crumble mix.

TIP

TO MAKE PLUM SKINS EASIER TO RE-MOVE, PLACE IN A BOWL OF HOT WATER FOR 1 MINUTE BEFORE PEELING. THIS WILL LOOSEN THE SKINS.

APPLE & SULTANA CREME BRULEE

Peter Reilly

Here is an updated version of the classic
Crème Brûlée – a rich dessert topped with
caramelised brown sugar. Apple and sultanas
give this recipe its original flavour.

PREPARATION TIME: 15 MINS +
CHILLING
COOKING TIME: 35-40 MINS
SERVES 6

I N G R E D I E N T S

450 G/1 LB DESSERT APPLES,
PEELED AND CHOPPED

2 TBLS LEMON JUICE

25 G/1 OZ SULTANAS

600 ML/1 PT DOUBLE CREAM

1 CINNAMON STICK

3 EGG YOLKS

50 G/2 OZ CASTER SUGAR

4 TBLS DEMERARA SUGAR

4 Divide the apple and sultana mixture equally between each of 6 ramekins. Divide the cream mixture between all of them, leave to cool then chill.

5 Top each ramekin with demerara sugar. Place under a fierce grill for 2-3 minutes, or until the sugar has melted and is bubbling on the top. Leave to cool, then chill for 1 hour before serving.

TIP

TO MAKE A CLASSIC CREME BRULEE ALL YOU HAVE TO DO IS OMIT THE APPLE AND SULTANA MIXTURE.

1 Put the apples, lemon juice and 4 tbls water in a pan. Cover and simmer over a gentle heat, stirring, for 15-20 minutes, until the apples have pulped. Stir in the sultanas and set aside.

2 Bring 450 ml/¾ pt of the cream to the boil with the cinnamon stick. Cover and set the mixture aside for 10 minutes then remove the cinnamon.

3 Whisk together the egg yolks and caster sugar until pale, then whisk in the remaining 150 ml/¼ pt cream. Stir this into the heated cream and cook, stirring, over moderate heat for 15 minutes until the mixture has thickened in the pan.

WATCHPOINT

IT IS IMPORTANT THAT THE GRILLING ELEMENT IS REALLY HOT. IF NOT, THE BRULEE MIXTURE WILL BEGIN TO MELT BEFORE THE SUGAR.

TARTE TATIN

Clint Brown

Probably one of the most famous of all French desserts, this upside-down apple tart is filled with sweet dessert apples and topped with golden caramel.

PREPARATION TIME: 15 MINS +
RESTING
COOKING TIME: 35-40 MINS
SERVES 4

INGREDIENTS

150 G/5 OZ SUGAR
50 G/2 OZ UNSALTED BUTTER
900 G/2 LB SMALL DESSERT APPLES, PEELED, CORED AND SLICED
25 G/1 OZ CASTER SUGAR
1 TSP COGNAC OR ARMAGNAC
175 G/6 OZ RICH SHORTCRUST PASTRY

3 Arrange the apples in alternate circles in the tin. Melt remaining butter in the frying pan, add the Cognac or Armagnac and then pour over the apples.

4 Roll out the pastry into a circle to fit the base of the tin. Lift the dough into the tin on top of the apples. Press down lightly.

1 Melt the sugar in a heavy-based pan with 4 tbls water over low heat until it caramelises. Pour the caramel carefully over the bottom of a 20 cm/8 in diameter, deep straight-sided cake tin, tilting the tin. Chill until hard.

5 Bake for 25-35 minutes, checking after 20 minutes that the pastry isn't browning too quickly – if it is, cover with foil. Remove from the oven, allow to cool for 5 minutes then invert onto a plate. Serve hot or warm.

TIP

THIS RECIPE TASTES JUST AS DELICIOUS MADE WITH SLIGHTLY UNRIPE PEARS, PEACHES OR APRICOTS.

2 Preheat the oven to 220 C/425 F/ Gas 7. Melt 25 g/1 oz butter and cook half the apples with half the caster sugar for 3 minutes. Transfer to a plate and cook remaining apples with remaining sugar.

JEWEL FRUIT TART

Paul Moon

Here's a summer pudding with a difference.
Take all the juicy fruits of summer, encase
them in a light-as-air pastry and you're ready
to enjoy this delicious Jewel Fruit Tart.

PREPARATION TIME: 40 MINS
+ CHILLING
COOKING TIME: 15-20 MINS
SERVES 6

INGREDIENTS

BUTTER, FOR GREASING

450 G/1 LB PUFF PASTRY

BEATEN EGG, FOR BRUSHING

100 G/4 OZ REDCURRANTS

100 G/4 OZ RASPBERRIES

100 G/4 OZ BLUEBERRIES

100 G/4 OZ STRAWBERRIES

100 G/4 OZ GREEN GRAPES

100 G/4 OZ APRICOTS, SLICED

3 TBLS APPLE JELLY

MINT SPRIGS, TO DECORATE

2 Roll out the pastry and lay over the template. Cut round the pastry with a knife and reserve off-cuts. Lay on a damp baking tray and brush around the edge with water. Cut 6 mm/¼ in wide strips from remaining pastry and position pieces around the edges of the main shape. Lay wider strips across the flower middle.

1 Preheat oven to 200 C/400 F/Gas 6. Make a pastry template. Cut out a 23 cm/9 in circle from a piece of greaseproof paper. Fold in half and then fold one corner two-thirds of the way over and bring the other over to cover it. Snip the corners off the curved edge. Unfold to give a flower shape with 6 sections. Grease well.

3 Cut pastry flower into 6 sections. Brush the top of the pastry strips with beaten egg. Prick the section bases with a fork. Chill the pastry in the fridge for 30 minutes.

4 Bake in the oven for 15-20 minutes until well risen and golden. Release the flan with a palette knife and cool. Prepare all of the fruit, arranging a different type of fruit in each section of the pastry flower.

TIP

IF FRESH FRUIT ISN'T READILY AVAILABLE, USE WELL-DRAINED CANNED OR FROZEN SUBSTITUTES.

5 Heat the apple jelly in a pan with 1 tbls water until liquefied. Pass through a sieve if necessary. Allow to cool slightly then spoon over the fruit. Decorate with mint sprigs.

Michael Michaels

APRICOT BAKEWELL

Chris King

Apricot Bakewell is a delicious variation on the
traditional British pudding recipe.
Halved apricots and cherries make a moist
filling as well as adding colour and flavour.

PREPARATION TIME: 30 MINS
COOKING TIME: 1 HOUR 50 MINS
SERVES 6

INGREDIENTS

375 G/13 OZ SHORTCRUST PASTRY,
THAWED IF FROZEN

2 TBLS APRICOT JAM

400 G/14 OZ TINNED APRICOT
HALVES, DRAINED

40 G/1½ OZ GLACE CHERRIES,
HALVED

100 G/4 OZ BUTTER

100 G/4 OZ CASTER SUGAR

2 EGGS

25 G/1 OZ SELF-RAISING FLOUR,
SIFTED

50 G/2 OZ GROUND ALMONDS

GRATED ZEST OF 1 LEMON

PINCH OF GROUND CINNAMON

2 TBLS MILK

25 G/1 OZ FLAKED ALMONDS

2 Spread the jam over the pastry base. Pat the apricots dry on kitchen paper. Place a halved cherry in each apricot half, then place cut side down on the jam. Cover the pastry case completely in this way.

3 Cream together the butter and sugar until light and fluffy. Beat in the eggs, one at a time, then fold in the flour, ground almonds, lemon zest, cinnamon and milk.

1 Preheat the oven to 200 C/400 F/ Gas 6. Roll out the pastry thinly and use it to line a 23 cm/9 in fluted flan tin. Prick the base with a fork.

Clive Streeter

TIP

COVER THE TOP OF THE APRICOT BAKE-
WELL WITH FOIL IF IT BROWNS TOO
QUICKLY DURING COOKING.

4 Spoon the cake mixture into the pastry case, smooth over the top then sprinkle on the almond flakes. Bake for 20 minutes then reduce the oven temperature to 180 C/350 F/ Gas 4 and cook for a further 1½ hours or until firm to the touch.

GOOSEBERRY TART

Nick Carman

The rings of gooseberries arranged on this tart hide a thick layer of set creamy custard. Serve chilled either as a dessert or with afternoon tea.

PREPARATION TIME: 30 MINS +
COOLING
COOKING TIME: 50 MINS
SERVES 6-8

I N G R E D I E N T S

200 G/7 OZ SHORTCRUST PASTRY,
THAWED IF FROZEN

2 TBLS CUSTARD POWDER

100 G/4 OZ CASTER SUGAR

300 ML/½ PT MILK

450 G/1 LB GOOSEBERRIES, TOPPED
AND TAILED

2 TBLS MARSALA

6 TBLS STRAINED GREEK YOGHURT

3 TBLS LIME JELLY MARMALADE

4 Place the custard in a liquidiser and blend with the Marsala. Scrape into a bowl and fold in the yoghurt. Spoon the custard into the pastry case and arrange the gooseberries on top.

1 Preheat the oven to 200 C/400 F/ Gas 6. Roll out the pastry to fit a 20 cm/8 in fluted flan ring. Bake blind for 25 minutes, then allow to cool on a wire rack.

2 Meanwhile place the custard powder and 2 tbls of the sugar in a bowl and blend in 2 tbls of the milk. Heat the remaining milk in a pan until it nears boiling point, then pour onto the slaked custard powder, stirring constantly. Return to the pan and heat, stirring·until thickened. Leave to cool.

5 Bring the gooseberry syrup to the boil. Boil rapidly for 5-10 minutes to reduce it by half. Stir in the marmalade until melted. Allow to cool slightly, then spoon over the gooseberry tart before serving.

TIP

DON'T USE FROZEN GOOSEBERRIES FOR THIS TART AS THEY GO SOGGY WHEN DEFROSTED AND LOOK UNATTRACTIVE.

SERVE CHILLED AND EAT WITHIN TWO DAYS AS THE CUSTARD WILL EVENTUALLY MAKE THE PASTRY SOGGY.

3 Place the gooseberries, 125 ml/ 4 fl oz water and the remaining sugar in a pan, cover and bring to the boil. Simmer for 5-10 minutes until soft. Remove and cool. Reserve syrup.

LEMON & ORANGE TART

Milk, cream and sugar help reduce the acidity
of the citrus fruit in this dish, producing
a bitter-sweet flavour and a rich, creamy
filling. Lemons provide the topping.

Preparation time: 25 mins
+ chilling
Cooking time: 50 mins
Serves 6-8

INGREDIENTS

350 G/12 OZ RICH SHORTCRUST
PASTRY

150 ML/¼ PT MILK

50 G/2 OZ SUGAR

2 EGG YOLKS

1 ½ TSP GELATINE

ZEST AND JUICE OF 1 LEMON

ZEST AND JUICE OF 1 ORANGE

150 ML/¼ PT DOUBLE CREAM

FOR THE TOPPING

3 LEMONS, THINLY SLICED

100 G/4 OZ SUGAR

dissolved; cool slightly then stir into the milk mixture. Add the orange and lemon zest and allow the mixture to cool.

4 Whip the double cream until soft peaks form, and then fold into the milk mixture. Pour into the lined flan tin and chill the tart until set.

1 Line a 24 cm/9½ in loose-based flan tin with pastry. Bake blind for 20 minutes in a hot oven. Remove the paper and beans and cook a further 5 minutes. Remove from the oven.

2 Heat the milk and 25 g/1 oz of the sugar to boiling point. Remove from the heat. Whisk together the remaining sugar and egg yolks until thick and creamy. Pour the hot milk over the egg yolk mixture, whisking. Return to the pan and heat, stirring, until thick enough to coat the back of the spoon, then cool.

3 Sprinkle the gelatine over the lemon and orange juice in a small pan. Heat gently until completely

5 Meanwhile make the topping: place lemons, sugar and 300 ml/ ½ pt water into a pan, bring to the boil and simmer for 15 minutes until the pith and zest are tender. Remove slices and drain on kitchen paper. Boil the remaining syrup rapidly for 5 minutes until thick, then cool. Arrange the lemons on top of the tart and glaze with the syrup.

TIP

IF YOU WANT TO MAKE PLAIN LEMON OR PLAIN ORANGE TARTS INSTEAD OF THE COMBINATION TART IN THE RECIPE, SUBSTITUTE THE ZEST AND JUICE OF 1 LEMON AND 1 ORANGE IN THE RECIPE ABOVE FOR THE ZEST AND THE JUICE OF 2 LEMONS OR 2 ORANGES.

PEAR & ARMAGNAC TART

Paul Moon

Juicy pears are delicious combined with this
Armagnac and cream sauce. The almond
pastry is totally different from shortcrust
because of its biscuit-like texture.

PREPARATION TIME: 25 MINS +
CHILLING
COOKING TIME: 50 MINS
SERVES 6-8

INGREDIENTS

4 DESSERT PEARS, PEELED, HALVED,
AND CORED

3 TBLS LEMON JUICE

5 TBLS ARMAGNAC

2 TBLS CASTER SUGAR

150 ML/¼ PT DOUBLE CREAM

FOR THE ALMOND PASTRY

225 G/8 OZ FLOUR

PINCH OF SALT

75 G/3 OZ GROUND ALMONDS

75 G/3 OZ CASTER SUGAR

2 EGG YOLKS

175 G/6 OZ UNSALTED BUTTER,
SOFTENED

1 Preheat the oven to 180 C/350 F/ Gas 4. Place the pear halves in a shallow ovenproof dish, and sprinkle with lemon juice to stop them going brown.

2 Pour 3 tbls of the Armagnac over the top, cover with foil and bake for 15-20 minutes until soft but still firm. Leave to cool.

3 Make the pastry: sift the flour and salt on to a work surface. Sprinkle with ground almonds and make a well in the centre. Gradually incorporate

the sugar and egg yolks then the butter. Knead lightly, wrap and chill in the fridge for 30 minutes.

4 Roll out half the pastry and line a 23 cm/9 in flan tin. Arrange the drained pears (save the liquid) in the tin with the narrow ends touching in the middle. Roll out the remaining pastry, cut a 5 cm/2 in circle from the middle and cover the pears. Brush with water and sprinkle with sugar.

5 Bake at 200 C/400 F/Gas 6 for 25-30 minutes or until the pastry is pale gold. Whip the cream until thick and beat in the cooking liquid with the rest of the Armagnac. Spoon into the middle of the pie while hot.

WATCHPOINT

TO PREVENT THE PASTRY FROM GETTING TOO BROWN WHEN COOKING, PUT A STRIP OF FOIL AROUND THE EDGE.

PINEAPPLE LATTICE TARTS

Ian O'Leary

To make these professional-looking tarts, all you need is a little patience. Once you've mastered the art of lattice cutting pastry, you won't be cross with the results!

PREPARATION TIME: 15 MINS
+ CHILLING
COOKING TIME: 25-30 MINS
MAKES 8-10

I N G R E D I E N T S

225 G/8 OZ TINNED PINEAPPLE
CHUNKS IN SYRUP

½ TBLS ARROWROOT

1 TBLS KIRSCH

400 G/14 OZ PUFF PASTRY, THAWED
IF FROZEN

3 Cut slits, 12 mm/½ in long, in staggered rows, 6 mm/¼ in apart in the remaining pastry. Gently pull apart the slits to make a lattice. Cut out 8-10 more rounds from the patterned pastry using a 9 cm/3½ in cutter.

1 Roughly chop the pineapple and tip into a pan with the syrup. Heat gently. Dissolve the arrowroot in the kirsch and stir into the pineapple. Cook until opaque. Remove from the heat. Allow to cool.

2 Roll out the pastry until it is 6 mm/ ¼ in thick. Using a 7.5 cm/3 in cutter or teacup, stamp out 8-10 rounds from half of the pastry.

4 Preheat the oven to 200 C/400 F/ Gas 6. Spoon about 1 tbls of the pineapple mixture onto each plain round, reserving 2 tbls of the sauce. Brush the edges with water and lay a lattice lid on top. Transfer to a baking tray and chill for 20 minutes. Brush the tops with the reserved sauce and bake the tarts for 20-25 minutes or until puffed up and golden.

TIP

MAKE A VARIETY OF FRUIT-FLAVOURED TARTS BY SUBSTITUTING ANY OTHER TINNED FRUIT OR PIE FILLING FOR THE PINEAPPLE. IF THE FRUIT IS LARGE, LIKE APRICOTS, PEACHES OR PEARS, CHOP IT UP INTO SMALL PIECES. IF THE FRUIT IS IN ITS OWN JUICE RATHER THAN SYRUP, YOU MAY WISH TO ADD A LITTLE SUGAR TO SWEETEN THE MIXTURE.

STRAWBERRY FILO GATEAU

Clint Brown

A fabulous concoction of Genoese sponge
layered with strawberries and cream,
decorated with the prettiest filo flowers.

PREPARATION TIME: 45 MINS
COOKING TIME: 45 MINS
SERVES 6

I N G R E D I E N T S

BUTTER, FOR GREASING

4 SHEETS FILO PASTRY

25 G/1 OZ BUTTER, MELTED

300 ML/½ PT DOUBLE CREAM

225 G/8 OZ STRAWBERRIES

ICING SUGAR, FOR DUSTING

FOR THE SPONGE

4 EGGS

115 G/4½ OZ CASTER SUGAR

115 G/4½ OZ FLOUR

PINCH OF SALT

50 G/2 OZ BUTTER, MELTED

1 Grease and base line a 20 cm/8 in spring-form tin. Preheat the oven to 190 C/375 F/Gas 5. For the sponge, put the eggs and sugar in a bowl over a pan of simmering water. Whisk until pale and mousse-like. Remove from the heat and whisk until cool.

2 Sift the flour with the salt. Fold half into the mixture. Pour the butter in a thin stream around the edge of the bowl and fold in, followed by the remaining flour. Pour into tin and bake for 35 minutes until golden and springy.

3 Allow the cake to cool in the tin for 5 minutes, then remove and cool completely on a wire rack.

Lay the filo sheets one on top of the other, brushing between each layer with melted butter. Cut out 6 x 6.5 cm/2½ in circles and dampen the centres with water. Pinch the centres together to make frilly flower shapes to decorate the gateau.

4 Cut out a circle from the remaining filo using the tin as a template. Place on a baking tray with the filo flowers and bake at 190 C/375 F/Gas 5 for 8-10 minutes. Cool.

Peter Reilly

5 Cut the cake into three layers. Whip the cream and spread one third onto each layer. Reserve 6 strawberries for decoration and cut the remaining fruit in half. Arrange on top of the cream on two layers and assemble the cake. Place the filo circle on top of the gateau and dredge with icing sugar. Arrange filo flowers around the top. Partly slice through the reserved strawberries to make fans and place in between the flowers. Dredge with more icing sugar and serve.

APPLE & CHERRY STRUDEL

JJ Crofton

A variation of the classic apple strudel,
bursting with cherries and sultanas and
finished with a dusting of icing sugar.

PREPARATION TIME: 20 MINS
COOKING TIME: 40-45 MINS
SERVES 8

INGREDIENTS

2 BRAMLEY APPLES, PEELED AND
DICED

75 G/3 OZ DEMERARA SUGAR

1 TSP GROUND CINNAMON

350 G/12 OZ TINNED OR FROZEN RED
CHERRIES, STONED

50 G/2 OZ SULTANAS

6 SHEETS OF FILO PASTRY

50 G/2 OZ BUTTER, MELTED, PLUS
EXTRA FOR GREASING

25 G/1 OZ ICING SUGAR

2 Lay the filo sheets out flat on a work surface. Brush each sheet with the melted butter and carefully layer the sheets into a pile.

1 Preheat the oven to 180 C/350 F/ Gas 4. Place the apples and 2 tbls water in a saucepan and cover. Bring to the boil and cook gently for 5 minutes until the apples have softened. Stir in the sugar cinnamon, cherries and sultanas, then remove from the heat.

3 Spread the apple mixture evenly over the pastry. Then carefully roll up the pastry away from you.

4 Lightly grease a baking tray. Place the strudel on the sheet and bake for 35-40 minutes, until golden. Remove from the oven and dust with icing sugar. Serve hot or cold in slices.

 IF YOU ARE USING FROZEN CHERRIES, DEFROST THOR-OUGHLY BEFORE COOKING.

TIP

SCORE THE PASTRY INTO SLICES BEFORE BAKING. THIS MAKES IT EASIER TO SLICE WITHOUT DAMAGING THE PASTRY, AFTER IT IS COOKED.

INDEX